Zooman and the Sign

By Charles Fuller

S A M U E L   F R E N C H , I N C.

45 West 25th Street   NEW YORK, N.Y. 10010
7623 Sunset Boulevard   HOLLYWOOD 90046
LONDON   *TORONTO*

ZOOMAN AND THE SIGN, by Charles Fuller; directed by Douglas Turner Ward; scenery designed by Rodney J. Lucas; lighting by Shirley Prandergast; costumes by Judy Dearing; production stage manager Clinton Turner Davis. Presented by the Negro Ensemble Company. Mr. Ward, artistic director and Gerald S. Krone, managing director. At Theater Four, 424 West 55th Street. Opening date was December 7, 1980. The cast was as follows:

ZOOMAN . . . . Giancarlo Esposito
RACHEL TATE . . . . Mary Alice
EMMETT TATE . . . . Carl Gordon
REUBEN TATE . . . . Ray Aranha
VICTOR TATE . . . . Alvin Alexis
RUSSELL ADAMS . . . . Terrance Terry Ellis
DONALD JACKSON . . . . Steven A. Jones
ASH BOSWELL . . . . Frances Foster
GRACE GEORGES . . . . Carol Lynn Maillard

Zooman And The Sign

ACT ONE

Scene 1

(*A LIVING-ROOM, middle class and fairly modern, though a bit ornate, occupies much of the stage. In the living-room, the furniture is comfortable. Beyond the living-room* UPSTAGE RIGHT *is the front door which leads out to a porch. The porch door opens onto a single stoop and the sidewalk, which operates* DOWN-STAGE, *across the entire stage front.* DOWNSTAGE RIGHT *is a medium sized raised platform on which an actor should be able to pace. A staircase* UPSTAGE LEFT *inside an archway corridor leads to the 2nd floor, and to the* RIGHT *of the living-room.* UPSTAGE *of the archway leads to an unseen dining-room and kitchen* OFFSTAGE. *The light rises slowly over the platform. In the spotlight standing on the platform is a young black Man. He steps forward, looking at the audience rather contemptuously. He is wearing a mesh and plastic green and white baseball cap tilted to the side. A red T-shirt, with the inscription "Me" on it, hangs outside a pair of slacks or dungarees designed with two large pockets, one on each side of the pants. He is wearing high top sneaks. There are several thin, gold and silver chains around his neck. He is* ZOOMAN *and is always accompanied when he Enters by a low, rather dissonant Disco sound. As he*

stands looking at the audience, his music fades slightly, but lingers in the BG. ZOOMAN *may carry a radio, but it is not necessary.*)
(ZOOMAN *enters* DOWNSTAGE LEFT, *crosses* STAGE RIGHT *on sidewalk with a stylized dance-walk "bobbing" movement in time to the music, to the platform* DOWNSTAGE RIGHT.)

ZOOMAN. Once upon a time, while the goose was drinkin' wine? Ole' monkey robbed the people on the trolley car line. (*Laughs.*) I carry a gun and a knife. A gun in this pocket — and ole' 'Magic' in this one! (*Takes out knife and flicks it open.*) Now you see it — (*Makes a stabbing gesture.*) Now you don't! (*Smiles.*) I cut a mothafucka' with this baby yesterday. Ole' foreigner walking on the subway platform. (*He waddles, amused.*) Arms swingin' all ova' everywhere — bumpin' into people — glasses, two, three inches thick standin' out from his eyes, can't half see! And I'm trying to listen to my music too? No-talking mothafucka' needed to get cut. (*Smiles.*) 'Magic' knicked him. 'Magic' is sharp as a razor. He ain't even know he was cut 'til he was halfway down the platform, and the blood started runnin' down the ole' punk's hand. (*Looks at the knife.*) Mothafucka' started screamin' — dropped his newspapa' — jumpin' up and down, pleadin' to everybody waitin' on the subway. Ain' nobody do nothin' — ole' jive West Indian mothafucka' damn near got hit by a train! (*Laughs.*) Fell all down on the ground and shit — peed on hisself! Shiiit, he wasn't hurt that bad! 'Magic' only knicked the scared mothafucka'! (*To himself, after a pause.*) Mothafucka' don't know what scared is! (*Crosses* S.L. *onto the* S.R. *sidewalk area; distinct change of mood.*) They call me, Zoo-man! That's right. Z-O-O-M-A-N! From the Bottom! I'm the runner' down thea'. When I knuck with a dude, I fight like a panther. Strike like a cobra! Stomp on mothafuckas' like a whole herd of Bi-son! Zooman! (*Irritated.*) That ole' mothafucka' yesterday coulda' put somebody's eye out. Swinging his arms around like he owned the whole fuckin' platform. Lotta' ole' people take advantage of you jes' cause they ole'. Movin' all slow and shit—mumblin' unda' they breath—(*Crosses* s.r. *onto his platform.*) shufflin' down the street all bent ova and twisted up—skin hangin' off they faces—makes my stomach turn jes' to look at 'em! I got an Aunt like that. Me and Kenny useta' stay to that mean bitch's house sometimes. Evil ole' skunk walkin' down the avenue, one mile an hour and shit, useta hit us across the mouth with a fly swatter jes' for talkin' at the mothafuckin' table! I was glad when the 'junkies' would steal her check. We useta' tell her, she was dumb for goin' down there—don't nobody with any sense walk on the 'Avenue' with a social-security check in they hands! (*To himself.*) Lotta' times we'd be to that bitch's house, three—four days, wouldn't eat nothin'. (*Casually crosses* s.l. *onto* s.r. *sidewalk.*) What am I doing here now? I just killed somebody. Little girl, I think. Me and Stockholm turned the corner of this street?—and there's Gustav and them jive mothafuckas' from uptown, and this litte bitch has to be sitting on her front steps playing jacks—or some ole' kid shit! But I had tol' Gustav if I eva' saw his ass around the 'Avenue,' I'd blow him away. (*Shrugs.*) So I started shootin' and she jes' got hit by one of the strays, that's all. She ain't had no business bein' out there. That street is a war zone—ain' nobody see her, we was runnin'—shit! And in that neighborhood you supposed to stay indoors, anyway! (*Pause.*) She was in the wrong place at the wrong time—how am I supposed to feel guilty over somethin' like that? Shiiit, I don't know the little bitch, anyway. (ZOOMAN *exits* s.r.)

(*The Lights begin to fade around* ZOOMAN *as his music comes up softly in the BG. Simultaneously, the light builds in the* TATE *living-room [as the scrim opens]. The* ZOOMAN *music fades. The mood is heavy. Action is continuous. On the sofa sits* RACHEL, *an attractive black woman.* REUBEN *is dressed in a bus driver's uniform,* RACHEL *in skirt and blouse. Uncle* EMMETT, *a man not much older than* REUBEN *is seated in an arm chair* S.L. *of sofa. Also there is* VICTOR, *the* TATE'S *15-year-old son. He is dressed surprisingly similar to* ZOOMAN. REUBEN, *standing* U. *to the sofa, attempts to comfort* RACHEL.)

RACHEL. I keep seeing her, Reuben—feeling her all over the room. And I want to say something to her—reach out and straighten her hair, touch her dress. And I know she's gone—

EMMETT. I say we go out there—me and your Reub, with two pistols, hunt the little bastards down and put a goddam bullet in each one of 'em's head! Look, these are kids that ain't *about* nothin', ain't *goin'* nowhea', and ain't *no* good—and I say let's cut our losses—(*Rises, crosses to imaginary window* D.L.) I don't mind tellin' people we've got treacherous black kids out there! But let's get rid of 'em, Reub!

REUBEN. Come on, Emmett! (*Crosses around the* S.R. *side of the sofa, and sits next to* RACHEL, *comforting her. To* RACHEL.) Try to relax, Baby.

EMMETT. (*Crosses Upstage to sofa to* S.R. *side of sofa.*) They just killed your daughter, Nephew—on her own front steps! You think anybody's gonna' look too hard for the boys who did it? Where you been? (*He is close to tears.*)

REUBEN. Who do we go out and kill?

EMMETT. All of 'em with their hats tipped to the side,

and them goddamn basketball sneaks on, that's who!

VICTOR. I wear sneaks, Uncle Emmett.

EMMETT. (*Quickly turns to* VICTOR.) Buy you a pair of loafers then boy!

RACHEL. (*Immediately.*) Emmett, will you please stop it? You're threatening my son. Just stop it! (*There is a brief silence in the house.*)

EMMETT. (*Hurt.*) I'm sorry—don't pay no attention to me! Tell her Reuben—he'll tell you Rachel, I always say too much. (*Crosses above sofa to arm chair.*) I ain't gonna' say nothin' else. (*He sits in the arm chair.*)

REUBEN. You can talk Emmett—but just stop that 'killin' business—we just saw Jinny stretched out on a table dead!

EMMETT. Alright—(*Slight pause.*) I guess y'all the bereaved family, huh? Well, I want you to know, I'm family too!

REUBEN. Nobody said nothin' about you not bein' in the family!

EMMETT. Y'all are not the only people gonna' miss her—I was her Godfather too, remember that! I carried her first bassinet down here on the train from New York. (*Rises and crosses* R. *above sofa to* S.R. *of sofa.*) You have any idea what losin' Jinny did to us? There ain't that many of us left! Five—and Ash is Rachel's kin! (*He points to* VICTOR.) That's the last Tate sittin' right there—and I'm not supposed to have something to say? (*Crosses* D.R. *to imaginary window.*) I'll tell you what: If they come back through here again with they little gangwar—I got something for 'em!

REUBEN. Come on Emmett—that's enough, now.

EMMETT. (*Crosses to* R. *of sofa.*) What's wrong with you? I can remember the time I'da had to hold him back—nobody messed with the Tates! Thing like this happen, your father and the rest of us would be on the street until we caught the little sons-a'-bitches, and took and eye for an eye!

REUBEN. We're not headhunters. This is not the old days! Emmett—you livin' in the past!

EMMETT. You changed when you got married.

REUBEN. Emmett, the next goddamn thing you say, I'm puttin' your ass back on the train to New York!

EMMETT. I just may go!

REUBEN. (*Rises.*) Then go, dammit!

RACHEL. Will y all stop it please? Please? All this wild talk is not gonna' bring Jinny back.

(EMMETT *crosses* S.L. *above sofa. There is a moment of silence.* REUBEN *crosses toward* EMMETT *and stands* U.R. *of sofa.*)

REUBEN. Why don't you get us both a beer, Emmett? It'll cool us off. Is there still beer in the box, Honey?

RACHEL. There's some in there.

REUBEN. Get me a cold one, OK?

Emmett. I still think I got a right to say something. (*Crosses* U.C. *of sofa. Softer.*) I'm sorry Rachel. And I didn't mean that about you, Victor. (*Exits* U.R. *to kitchen.* REUBEN *sits* S.R. *sofa.*)

VICTOR. What was Uncle Emmett talkin' about, Dad?

REUBEN. Aw, mess happened before you was born. I was boxing then. Stuff not worth repeatin'. (*To* RACHEL.) You all right?

RACHEL. (*Nods.*) Got a slight headache, though.

REUBEN. Did you take any aspirins?

RACHEL. (*Nods.*) But too many of them, and they work on my stomach. (REUBEN *reaches for her.*) I'm all right—but it just happened . . . and it's hard to get over, Reuben!

REUBEN. (*Gently.*) Rachel, come on now—

VICTOR. Can I go out?

RACHEL. (*Suddenly terrified.*) No!

REUBEN. Relax!

RACHEL. Where's he gonna go? Out on the same street, so they can kill him, too? (*To* VICTOR.) No! You stay in here—we just got back into the house. You just stay in.

VICTOR. (*Rises, crosses to sofa.*) I wanna go out, Mom!

RACHEL. I said, no!

VICTOR. Just on the front steps—I want to be by myself!

RACHEL. We need to be together at a time like this—your father's here—

REUBEN. (*Firmly, overlapping.*) Go out, son. (VICTOR *rises quickly.*)

RACHEL. I don't want him out there, Reuben.

REUBEN. He's got a right to his own way of handling this thing, Rachel! (*To* VICTOR.) You heard me, son; go 'head! (*To* RACHEL.) Everybody's got their own way—(VICTOR *crosses hesitantly to front door, opens it.*)

REUBEN. Let him grieve any way he wants to.

RACHEL. Let him grieve in this house and live! (VICTOR *opens the screen door.*)

RACHEL. Victor!

VICTOR (*Stopping.*) What?

REUBEN. Dammit, leave him alone, Rachel.

RACHEL. (*After a pause.*) Well, he better not get off those steps then—(*Loud, To* VICTOR.) You stay around those steps out there, Victor! You hear me? In fact, don't go off the steps!

REUBEN. (*Shaking his head.*) Stay around the steps, son.

VICTOR. All right. (*Closes front door, closes screen door, crosses* D.S. *on porch, sits on porch steps.*)

RACHEL. That's right—around those steps. (*She is quiet for a moment, then rises and crosses* U.L. *to bookcase. Looks at picture of Jinny.*) This morning, she got up—took her forever to get her clothes on. She messed around with her food—started an argument with Victor—broke the last of those glasses I got from Ash. I told her I was going to call you if she kept it up. (*Crosses* D.L. *to 'window'.*) But I made her go outside, Reuben—I made her!

REUBEN. This is not your fault.

RACHEL. (*Crosses to* R. *window.*) She just got on my nerves so bad—She wouldn't listen! I told her three times to clean up that mess she left in her room—three times! (*Quietly.*) You shoulda' been here.

REUBEN. I'm here now—and I was here the weekend—

RACHEL. (*Interrupting.*) Are you going to stay this time—or leave—or what? (*Crosses* L. *below sofa to* D.L. *chair.*) because I really can't take it, Reuben! It's too much to ask me to do by myself right now—(EMMETT *enters* U.R. *with 3 cans of beer and crosses* U.C. *to sofa.* REUBEN *rises.*)

RACHEL. I can't deal with this and not know what's on your mind! (REUBEN *and* RACHEL *stop abruptly.* REUBEN *crosses* D.R. *to 'window'.* RACHEL *turns away.*)

EMMETT. (*Noticing, he crosses to Rachel and gives her a can of beer.* REUBEN *crosses* U.S. *to* S.R. *window.*) I brought you some beer, Rachel—it's cool, in this heat it'll make you feel better—(*Crosses to* REUBEN *and gives him a can of beer.*) Vic didn't leave on account of me, did he?

REUBEN. No.

EMMETT. Good! It's got to be tough on him, too! (RACHEL *crosses to sofa, sits.*)

EMMETT. You know they startin' to sell Budweiser on the trains now? (REUBEN *and* RACHEL *sip.*) They're nice and cold, Reub!

RACHEL. Thank you Emmett — I'm just — (EMMETT *crosses to* RACHEL, *stands above sofa, comforts her.*)

RACHEL. (*Leans back saddened again.*) I just feel so damn empty! (EMMETT *crosses* U.L. *to bookcase.*) I keep expecting her to come stomping down the stairs — or hear her disco music playing through that upstairs hall! How do you get used to an empty room? (*Pause.*) Reuben? (RACHEL *places beer can beside her on the floor.*) You remember the time she put on all my make up? You shoulda seen her that day, Emmett — lipstick from one end of her face to the other — rouge everywhere — powder in her hair — cologne all over her dress — (*Shakes her head.*) She was so much a girl!

REUBEN. (*Crosses to end table* S.R. *of sofa.*) Don't make yourself upset, baby —

RACHEL. I want to remember! She was born February 10, weighed 8 and ½ pounds, and had a star-shaped birthmark on the heel of her right foot — (*To herself.*) I don't know why she had that — I don't have one — and she didn't cry right away when they slapped her — did you know that, Emmett? (EMMETT *seems embarrassed; places beer* S.R. *end table.*) When Reuben first saw her, he said she looked like my side of the family, didn't you, Reuben? And she was easier than Victor. It was almost like she couldn't wait to pull herself out of me.

REUBEN. (*Crosses around sofa to* RACHEL.) Rachel.

RACHEL. I'm all right. I was just telling Emmett what I remember, he don't mind.

REUBEN. I think you should lay down.

RACHEL. I can't rest! How can I rest? Or just take aspirins? I keep seeing her crossing the room, Reuben — sitting in that chair — or that one! Or coming through the door.

REUBEN. (*Gestures to* EMMETT.) Baby, you hafta' lay down — Emmett, help me. (EMMETT *places his can of beer on floor* D.S. *of arm chair then crosses to* RACHEL. *He takes her left arm,* REUBEN *takes her right arm. They help her stand.*)

RACHEL. She's the baby, Reuben — how could they take the baby? (RACHEL *begins to cry as* REUBEN *and* EMMETT *reach for her.*)

REUBEN. Rachel, come on now — (*They cross around the left side of sofa to the hall* U.C. *and stand at the foor of the steps.*) I want you to lay down. Don't argue, you need the rest. You'll feel better.

RACHEL. (*Nods and begins to climb the stairs..*) Yes, I need the rest. (REUBEN *guides her up the stairs. She stops and turns to* REUBEN.) You call Ash.

REUBEN. Called her when we first got in. She's on her way. (RUSSELL, *a friend of* VICTOR's *enters* S.L., *sees* VICTOR *and slowly starts in his direction.* EMMETT *crosses to* D.S. *to the arm chair and picks up his beer. Sits.*)

RACHEL. She loves Jinny so much. I'm glad you're home, Reuben.

REUBEN. Shhh! You just hold onto me. (*They move up slowly.*)

RUSSELL. (*Stopping at the steps.*) Hey blood!

VICTOR. Hey, Russ.

RUSSELL. I'm sorry about your sista' man. (*Slight pause. He crosses* S.R., *looks onto porch. Turns to* VICTOR, *secretively.*) Word is, it was two dudes from the Bottom.

VICTOR. Who?

RUSSELL. (*Shrugs.*) But a dude named ZOOMAN runs it downtown. They say he's a little crazy. Tommy tol' me, Zooman and his brother Kenny beat up they own Mom — said they caught her comin' out the bar, and dusted her. That's his own mother! (VICTOR *is silent. Stands, pulls* RUSSELL *to his left;* S.L. *of porch.*)

VICTOR. (*Finally, to* RUSSELL.) Can you get me a gun?

RUSSELL. (*Surprised.*) You want a 'burner'? (VICTOR *nods.*) I guess I know how you feel, Vic — but Ward got the bullets.

VICTOR. Can you get the gun now?

RUSSELL. (*Nods.*) It'll take awhile though. I hide it in my Mom's room and she's been in bed sick since they shot — you know, since the shooting. It really shook her up, man. (REUBEN *enters slowly. Crossing down the stairs, he enters living-room, crosses to the end table and picks up his beer.*)

RUSSELL. Everybody around here like Jinny. (VICTOR *crosses onto porch.*) You goin' in? (VICTOR nods.) I'll see you later — I'll git it though. (RUSSELL *starts away.*) (VICTOR *enters the living-room; closes the front door and sits on window seat quietly.* RUSSELL *exits* S.L. *As* VICTOR *enters,* EMMETT *rises, crosses to* D.R. *'window'.* REUBEN *crosses* U.S. *of sofa, to* D.L. *window. Both look out. A quiet settles over things. Awkwardly* REUBEN *and* EMMETT *try to talk.*)

REUBEN. How was the trip from New York?

EMMETT. Same. How's the Bus company?

REUBEN. (*Shaking his head.*) They call theyself upgradin' the system . . . got all new buses. (EMMETT *crosses, sits* S.R. *sofa, places beer can from floor on* R. *end table.*) The old ones had that handle — you reached over, threw the handle forward and the front doors opened. (REUBEN *crosses, sits in arm chair.*) When the last person got off the bus in the back, the back doors swung back into position, shut and locked. But these new buses—you got one button to operate the whole system. And the damn thing never works—I have to get out of my seat, walk to the back of the bus and slam the right side of the back door before the damn thing will close! And they call that progress!

EMMETT. Ain't no different at Bellevue—they hire all these no-readin' niggahs, instead of teachin' 'em somethin'—and the otha' day, this kid been in my section 'bout four—five weeks, takes a bottle of acid off the shelf—how it got there I'll never know—pours it into a bucket, and damn if he don't start moppin' the floor with it! The damn tiles started turnin' brown—couple nurses shoes start burnin'. I caught it, but you know he told me he couldn't read—imagine that? Couldn't tell the difference between cleanin' compound and acid cause the two bottles look alike.

REUBEN. When do you have to go back to New York?

EMMETT. They told me I might have to be back Wednesday—it's vacation time, and I'm on call—plus most of those Brothers I'm workin' with don't know nothin' 'bout cleanin' hospital floors! Average one of 'em ain't neva even picked up a mop! (*Pause.*) What about you?

REUBEN. The Union gets us a week for something like this—it's the contract. (EMMETT *nods, and* REUBEN *is quiet.*)

EMMETT. (*Cutting across everything loudly, rises and crosses to* REUBEN.) I wanna do something Reuben! Goddamnit!

REUBEN. (*Shoots back.*) What? What Emmett? Kill somebody? Damnit, let it be! (*Tries to calm.*) There's nothin' to do! Leave it to the police—them boys ran through here in broad daylight! (*Rises and crosses* D.L..) EMMETT. When you ever know the police to catch anybody, when you the victim?

VICTOR. (*Rises, crosses* U.S. *of sofa.*) I'ma go upstairs, Dad.

REUBEN. Alright, go ahead, Son. (REUBEN *crosses* U.C. *to* VICTOR, *places his arm around* VICTOR'S *shoulders. They cross to the foot of the stairs.* EMMETT *crosses to* S.R. *window, looks onto porch.*) Vic, how are you doing?

VICTOR. Alright.

REUBEN. Look in on your mother, OK? (VICTOR *nods and starts upstairs, turns.*)

VICTOR. Are you gonna' stay, Dad?

REUBEN. I'll be here. (VICTOR *continues up. There is a brief silence.* REUBEN *crosses* U.C. *of sofa.*)

EMMETT. When did you and Rachel start havin' problems?

REUBEN. Four-five months now.

EMMETT. All the times I called you niggahs on the phone, and you ain't neva' said nothin' about it?

REUBEN. Emmett, goddamnit, it's none of your business!

EMMETT. It is my business! (EMMETT *crosses above sofa to* REUBEN.) I'm in this family—it is my business! (DONALD JACKSON *enters* S.R. *and crosses onto the front porch to the front door.*)

REUBEN. This is not the time to talk about it!

EMMETT. Y'all don't need no advice? You know everything?

(*The doorbell rings almost as a reprise. No-one moves at first.* REUBEN *and* EMMETT *share looks at one*

another. The strain is beginning to take its toll of
REUBEN. *The doorbell rings again.* REUBEN *holds*
back his own tears, and crosses D.L. *Sits in* D.S.L.
chair.)

REUBEN. (*Gently.*) Let me be, Emmett. (EMMETT
nods. He is ashamed of himself.)

EMMETT. (*Rises and starts to the door.*) I'll get it. (*He*
goes to the door as REUBEN *sits quietly in his own grief.*
EMMETT *glances back at* REUBEN *before opening the*
door.) Yes?

JACKSON. Hello, I'm Donald Jackson — I live down
the street? I just came by to see if there was anything I
could do?

EMMETT. (*Awkwardly.*) Come in — (EMMETT *opens*
the screen door. JACKSON *enters.*) Reub, Mr. Jackson's
here — I'm Emmett Tate, Reuben's Uncle. (*The two men*
shake.)

REUBEN. (*Recovering, overlapping.*) Hey, Jackson.
(*Rises.*) Come on in.

(JACKSON *takes a few steps past the door and crosses.*
Sits on the sofa. EMMETT *closes front door, sits on*
window seat.)

REUBEN. 'Xcuse the place.

JACKSON. It's all right Reub. I been knowin' y'all since
you moved 'round here — you don't have to be fancy
with me! (*To* EMMETT.) I useta' be a fan of his, when he
boxed light-heavy — and — I took his missus to the
hospital, when the little girl was born. Didn' I Reub?
(REUBEN *nods.*) My wife, she come and got me that
day — it was cold, I remember that — Reub was workin' —
(*There is a slight pause.*) They got me workin' split-shift

this week—I go on nights next Thursday—and I tol' my wife I'd just come over for a hot minute, Reub, to see if there was anything I could do.

REUBEN. I appreciate it, Jackson.

JACKSON. My wife, she was in the back hangin' clothes when it happened. By the time she got to the front door, them boys was halfway up the block. She didn't see nothin'—and me, I was at work, Reub—but my wife said there was something y'all might want to know—

REUBEN. (*Quickly.*) What? (REUBEN *places beer on floor next to chair.*)

JACKSON. Well—see by us livin' down at the end of the block, they got to us last—(*To* EMMETT.) See my house is actually on Master Street, but we never used that door—we always come out on the Titan Street side—it makes my house seem like the first house at that end of the street. Anyway, he didn't tell me, he told my wife, and she tol' me to tell Reuben. Cop told her he went to every house on the block and not one person claim they saw anything.

REUBEN. What!

JACKSON. That's what the cop said.

REUBEN. (REUBEN *rises and crosses to* S.L. *side of sofa.*) There's forty-fifty families around here!

JACKSON. It seemed strange to my wife, too, 'cause she said when she came outside, everybody in the block was on their porch. About half on your side, and most of them on my side.

REUBEN. You sure that's what the cop said? (JACKSON *nods.*) And they covered every house?

EMMETT. (*Rises, looks out window.*) They ain't shit, Reub!

REUBEN. That's impossible. Mrs. Smith sits on her

porch morning til night. Davis stays at his window—he
can't even get upstairs. (*Crosses to* D.L. *'window'.*) I
don't believe it!

RACHEL. (*Enters, crossing down the stairs unnoticed.*)
Believe what?

REUBEN. (*Answering reflexively.*) Nobody on the
block says they saw anything.

RACHEL. What! They can't—they're lying!

REUBEN. (*Realizing it's her.*) Rachel, you shouldn't
be up—

RACHEL. (*Crosses* U.S. *to sofa.*) I don't care what they
say, they're lying! I saw them. They were all out there!

REUBEN. (*Crosses to* RACHEL.) Maybe they too
shocked to talk yet.

RACHEL. (*Crosses to* S.R. *window.*) They'll tell me! I
saw them. Mrs. Smith, Julius Williams—

REUBEN. (*Crosses* S.R. *to* RACHEL.) Rachel—

RACHEL. (*Crosses to* D.R. *window.*) I saw Mrs. Smith
standing by her front door. I looked right at Julius
Williams—and Davis, Mr. Cortez, ole' man Washing-
ton!

REUBEN. Come on, Baby—(*Crosses to* RACHEL.
RACHEL *pulls away.* VICTOR *enters, crosses down the
stairs, unnoticed.*)

RACHEL. (*Crosses to* L. *window.*) Dottie Henson was
hanging out her window! They're not blind! Let me talk
to them—(*Crosses* S.R. *to* REUBEN. *He stops her.*) I'm
her mother! They'll talk to me! They'd better tell me! I
swear before God they betta tell me!

REUBEN. Stop it, Rachel!

RACHEL. No! They wouldn't dare lie to me! (*Pulls
away from* REUBEN, *crosses to* D.L. *'window'; shouts.*) I
saw you, Dottie!

REUBEN. (*Crosses to* RACHEL.) Rachel!

RACHEL. (*Turns to* REUBEN. *He tries to calm her down.*) I saw the bitch, Reuben! How can she say she didn't see it? They've got to tell me! They all saw it. They were all outside when those boys ran through here! They all watched her die!

REUBEN. Rachel . . . Rachel . . . (RACHEL *breaks down crying as* REUBEN *attempts to restrain and comfort her.*)

RACHEL. Goddamnit, I saw them! I saw them! I saw them . . .

(REUBEN *continues to hold* RACHEL *as the lights go down in the* TATE *residence and simultaneously* ZOOMAN's *music begins to rise. The scrim closes. The light builds over the platform, where* ZOOMAN *is squatting. He is playing with his gun, and almost listening to the music, when it begins to fade, he is almost pleasant.*)

ZOOMAN. When you got nothin' to do, come to the Zoo! (*Quieter.*) First couple hours are the worse. The big blue fools are probably sweeping the neighborhood by now, picking-up everybody in sight. So there ain't that many mothafuckin' places to hide — except maybe in a junkie-hole — or out here in the mothafuckin' park — (*Pause.*) I got someplace to go. I just don't wanna git nobody in trouble, that's all! You stay away from your people as long as you can — besides, my Mom neva' could take pressure, no way! She'd just sit there and cry — plus, it's the first damn place, the mothafuckin' Man is gonna' look! I ain't that dumb! (*Sudden mood swing.*) I shot the little bitch 'cause I felt like it! Zooman felt like shooting somebody! And that mothafuckin' Gustav is just lucky it ain't him! I got up this morning and felt like killing somebody! So what? (*Beat. He crosses to sidewalk.*) I got picked up 21 times last year! Everytime somebody black did somethin' and the cops didn't have a name? They busted me! Fuck y'all! Y'all don't lock up them dirty derelicts on the street—shit smellin' mothafuckas' hair all caked with grease and slime—sleepin' in cardboard boxes, siftin' through trash, talking to theyself—Beggin'! I try to set one of them filthy mothafuckas' on fire, every chance I get! (*Pause.*) Jive cunt call herself a teacher and come to school with her titties showin' everyday, in an all boys school—(*Crosses to* s.r. *platform.*) then gonna' talk shit, when they raped her. I was in Juvenile "D" 18 months. And I wasn' even in it! Here's a bitch been in the school three years, and ain't neva' looked at nobody! All young niggahs look alike! So me and Stockholm do time because a schoolteacher can't pick out the right boys—from her own fuckin' class, in a lineup! (*Crosses to* s.l. *sidewalk.*) And Stockholm's a niggah with straight hair! Bitch neva' taught us nothin'—but she's still there! They shoulda killed the bitch—then theyda' caught the right people. (*Pause.*) Tomorrow's *my* little sista's birthday! Not my sista' here—a half sista in Birmingham—she'll be ten. She's down there with my fatha's people. I gotta' 'notha half-sista' who's married. I got people everywhere. Detroit. California. I got an Uncle in Buffalo—couple cousins in Houston. I got a Aunt on my motha's side graduated top of her class at college—Plus I got friends in town! PJ—Mooky, Christine—so I got plenty of places to go if I want to! Plenty. (*Pause.*) I just don't want to.

(*The light fades around* Zooman, *simultaneously with the lights building on the* Tate *household. The*

scrim closes. It is after midnight and though dark,
the house seems less troubled than before, due
mostly to a smallish woman, thin, in her late fifties.
Her name is ASH BOSWELL *and like* RACHEL, *she is*
dressed in a robe. But there the similarity stops.
ASH *is stylish and for her age, a good-looking*
woman; her hair is done, her makeup in place
despite the hour. REUBEN *sits on sofa.* RACHEL *sits*
in armchair. ASH *stands upstage of armchair, her*
hands on RACHEL's *shoulders. The phone is ringing*
and ASH *picks it up as scene begins.*)

ASH. Hello? Yes—no, this is her Cousin—unhuh—it
was a shock for everybody—unhuh. I'll tell them.
Thanks for calling. (*Hangs up.*) Somebody named
Mason—lives down the street. (ASH *hangs phone up,*
crosses D.S. *to* RACHEL.)

REUBEN. I'm tellin' you Rachel it was like they didn't
know me! Mr. Davis, and Gibson down the street? They
didn't even answer the door! And I could hear Gibson
draggin' that bad leg of his across the floor! His screen
door was closed but his front door was wide open—the
TV was on! I go down the street to Julius Williams'
house, and he acts like he didn't know we *had* a
daughter! Not one damn person on the block claims
they saw anything! The woman Rachel saw leanin' out
her window, Dottie Henson—and that boy Russell's
mother claim they didn't even hear the shots!

RACHEL. They're lying!

REUBEN. I know.

ASH. It's a shame how we Negroes have changed
through the years, Honey—from one extreme to the
next, like Jekyll and Hyde! (*Pause.*) How was that Uncle of yours when you passed through the dining-room?

REUBEN. He's sleeping.

RACHEL. He drank quite a bit while you were gone.

ASH. Got sassy too, didn't he? (*Winks at* RACHEL. *Crosses* S.R. *above sofa.*) If he wasn't family — a couple of those times he got out of hand, ole' Ash woulda' popped him upside his head! He's younger than I am by seven months, you know, so I can straighten his butt out quick, Honey! (*Slight pause.*) But I knew he was taking it pretty bad when I walked in here — he needs his sleep. You Tates get evil when you drink, Honey. (*Crosses around sofa; sits* S.R. *side.*) That's something we don't have on the Boswell side. (*Laughs, but* REUBEN *is distracted.* REUBEN *rises and crosses to* D.R. *'window'.* ASH *notices.*) What's the matter, Reuben?

REUBEN. It's these people. What happens if the police catch the boys they think did it, and nobody comes forward to identify them? They go free?

ASH. Black people don't like to deal with the police, Reuben.

REUBEN. I'm not the police! (*Crosses to* D.R. *of sofa.*) Me and Rachel been livin' here 15 — 16 years! Jinny was born on this block! And they all act like strangers — what's wrong with them? (*Crosses to* D.R. *'window'.*) All I've done for these people — Simpson, Edwards! Loaned Davis my tools — took him to the hospital — and I know he saw it! He sits in front of that goddamn window of his all day! The man's a cripple! — and in the summertime around here, you can't *get* these Negroes off they porches!

ASH. I blame a lot of this on them food stamps, Honey.

REUBEN. (*Crosses* U.S. *of sofa.*) Food stamps?

ASH. That's right! When the 'Negro' was hungrier, we treated each other better. Nowadays everybody's got their bellies full and we sit up belchin', watching those damn Soap Operas and Game Shows all day—hot dog in one hand, the phone in the other, a beer—or a Pepsi on the floor beside us—the baby crawlin' around dirty, the whole house filthy, and honey don't give a damn about nobody! You hear me? (*Slight pause.*) When we knew we might have to borrow a cup of flour—or a pair of pants—or a white shirt from the people across the street, we were a lot more concerned about them, and a lot more conscientious about ourselves.

REUBEN. Now Ash—

ASH. What else is it, then? There was a time when you didn't see black girls in their teens and early twenties, fat and out of shape, honey! No indeed! Those food stamps got all these children eatin' cookies, candy and potato-chips! A woman reached her forties and fifties you'd understand the weight, but when I was young honey, we took care of our figures—humph! Our bustlines and hips were legendary.

RACHEL. (*Gently.*) But Ash, Reuben's—talking about somethin' else.

ASH. It's all the same—if they don't care about themselves, their own health, how they gonna' care about you? Or Jinny or any of it?

REUBEN. It's not food stamps, all right? (*Crosses to* s.r. *window.*) Not one food stamp answered anybody's door on this block, Ash! (ASH *rises, a little hurt.*)

ASH. I'll finish the dishes.

RACHEL. Just leave them, Ash. (*To* REUBEN.) You didn't have to holler, Reuben.

REUBEN. I'm sorry, Ash.

ASH. It's all right. (*Crosses to* REUBEN.) I know what kind of time this is—besides, I need to do something with my hands—take my mind off things. (*Saddens.*)

It's still hard for me to accept it. When your call came, I just sat in a chair beside the window thinking about her. Remember that time she came up to Boston? She went off in those people's hearts like a firecracker. My Pastor, Rev. Daniels? He loved her—still talks about what a beautiful child she was. (*Suddenly distracted.*) That reminds me, I'd better call him and ask him to send somebody over to my house. When I got up, I just ran out and jumped in the car—I'm not even sure I closed all the windows. (*Starts away.*) But it's a shame is what it is—(*She exits and the room is quiet for a moment.*)

RACHEL. Did you have any trouble getting away this afternoon?

REUBEN. (*Shakes head 'no'.*) I told Sid the foreman what happened and he let me go right away. How come you didn't go to work?

RACHEL. Inventory. They're bringing in the fall line—changing displays. Sometimes that department store is like a Zoo. (*Long pause.*) Are you still seeing Florence?

REUBEN. I was never *seeing* Florence—I was with the woman one time!

RACHEL. I don't want to know about it!

REUBEN. You saw me with her—I told you I was sorry about that six months ago! I'm livin' in one room Rachel, with one bed, one pillow—

RACHEL. I don't want my husband to be with other women!

REUBEN. (*Crosses to R. of sofa.*) I'm not going to say it no more—I'm not with no otha' woman.

RACHEL. (*To herself.*) You better not be! (*Slight pause.*) I don't want my husband to do that—and I'm not saying you're not a good person—or good father. You do for us—the children love you and I love you, but I'll be damned if I let you live here with me and run around with other women! You are not going to do that to me!

REUBEN. I can't keep apologizing for it!

RACHEL. And I can't take it—not that and this too! I can't!

REUBEN. Then let it be! I feel bad enough, Rachel. I wasn't even here when it happened—I feel bad enough! (*Crosses* U.C. *to foot of stairs. The room is quieter.* RACHEL *softens.*)

RACHEL. Jinny asked me yesterday if she could call you.

REUBEN. She called—she said you told her it was all right. I was glad you did that.

RACHEL. How did she sound?

REUBEN. Like Jinny, her mouth going non-stop, (*Crosses to sofa.*) told me all about this new record she bought by the Commodores—and some book you said she could read, that was sexy, but not sexy enough for me to worry about—(*Sits* S.L. *sofa arm.*) was she that old?

RACHEL. She had her first period a couple of weeks ago—you know what she said? Said she didn't like the blood—it got all over everything, and did I think it would ever happen without all the blood. (*Pause.*) She was laying in it, Reuben—it was all over the steps—and I wanted to save it—bring her back to life!

REUBEN. Try not to think about it. (*He grabs her and holds her for a moment as she fights back tears, and nods, taking several breaths. She is quiet for a moment.*)

RACHEL. She said she wanted us back together again.

REUBEN. She said it to me too—I'm not going anywhere.

RACHEL. Reuben, why don't we move? We could spend more time together—I took the kids out to that shopping-center out on Route 452? It's nice out there! And we're both working—this place is almost paid for, and in a few years if we stay, we won't be able to get our money back!

REUBEN. You know we can't move—the porch isn't paid for—we got a 225 dollar car note—and it's week to week around here!

RACHEL. I don't want to live here anymore! (*Rises, crosses to* D.R. *'window'.* REUBEN *stands.*) You can't walk the streets—I'm sick of it! And nobody gives a damn! I even had to call the police myself—leave my baby and go to the phone, because I didn't hear a siren! They stood on their porches with their mouths open! What if it had been Grace's little girl, Denise? Or Mr. Davis' granddaughter Phyllis? (*Crosses to* REUBEN.) Reuben, I want to move!

REUBEN. We can't go anywhere, until somebody around here says they saw something.

RACHEL. (*Pulls away from* REUBEN, *crosses to* D.R. *'window'.*) What are you gonna' do, drag them outta' their houses?

REUBEN. Emmett wasn't all wrong, in the old days I'da got them to say something or kicked their damned doors in!

RACHEL. And what would that prove?

REUBEN. I'm her father! I can't just sit here and do nothing!

RACHEL. Reuben, you promised me—(*Crosses to* REUBEN.) you're not a fighter anymore, you're a bus-driver—

ASH. (*Enters with apron on, potato and potato peeler in hand. Stands* U.C..) You all call me?

REUBEN. (*Quieter.*) No, Ash—(*He stares at* RACHEL, *a little frustrated.*)

ASH. I'm making potato salad, Rachel.

RACHEL. Ash, I don't want all that food! (*Crosses to* S.R. *window.*) All the family we have is here, and I don't want these people in this neighborhood in my house, slopping down my food and staggering home drunk! We don't need any potato salad!

ASH. You don't need what?

RACHEL. (*Crosses to sofa, sits.*) You think I want them in my living-room, sitting on my furniture—

ASH. (*Crosses to* D.S.R. *sofa.*) I never heard of a black family in mourning in my life that didn't have potato salad for people who come by to pay their respects. Never in my life! It's bad manners! What are people supposed to eat?

REUBEN. (*Turns to* ASH.) Make the potato salad, Ash.

ASH. (*Nods.*) Where's the relish?

REUBEN. I think it's in the refrigerator—in those shelves on the door.

ASH. (*Starts out, shaking her head; to herself.*) I never heard of that in my life! (*Exits* U.R..)

(*There is a long pause.* REUBEN *and* RACHEL *stare at one another for awhile, but* RACHEL *breaks their silence with a sudden painful outburst.*)

RACHEL. (*On the verge of tears.*) Reuben, tell me it's not so. Please tell me it's not so. I think I'm just gonna' explode and die in a minute! And keep exploding—and dying, and dying—over, and over, and over—(REUBEN *crosses to* RACHEL, *sits* S.L. *of her on the sofa; attempts to comfort her.*) My stomach's sour, Reuben! Where she was in my stomach is empty! And I'm sick! God, I'm so sick! I'm so sick!

(*The lights begins to fade around the* TATE *household as the scrim closes, and rise slowly over the platform along with* ZOOMAN'S *music.* ZOOMAN *steps slowly on to the platform, smiling.*)

ZOOMAN. You know, I damn near got caught? I go snatch this ole' bitch's pocketbook, and she started yellin'—wig came off, and shit! I had to knock her down! Then this hero mothafucka' chases my ass five blocks before I could duck into an all night movie. (*Shakes head.*) And sure enough, the Big Blues comes walking down the aisle shinin' a flash light in everybody's face—and all these nasty mothafuckas' with their flies open started jumpin' up coverin' their faces, cause the Big Blues came in while this bitch on the screen is screwing four dudes, and half the scum in the movie has their fucky ass dicks out! (*Disgusted.*) Sick mothafuckas'! I acted like I had dropped somethin' but the Man stood *right* there, 'til I straightened up—(*Crosses onto* S.R. *sidewalk.*) but just then this crazy Brother down front leaps up, starts shoutin' at the screen—"The day of judgment is coming! The day of judgment is coming!" Ran all up on the stage, waving a gun—calling' everybody filth—and the Big Blues took off after him. (*To himself.*) I'm glad I got rid of that gun. 'Magic' is all I need anyway. (*Opens switchblade.*) You shoulda' seen that bitch when I stuck it in her face—she was lucky her pocketbook was all I took. You ain't expect me to eat out of no garbage can, did you?

(*Chuckles.*) Bitch screamed her fuckin' head off! Help!
Thief! (*Crosses to* s.r. *platform. Pause.*) But they ain't
caught Zooman yet. And they may never catch me.

(*Lights fade slowly around* ZOOMAN *along with his
music as he exits* s.r. *and comes up on the sidewalk
area.* REUBEN *enters* s.l., *crossed* d.s. *to sidewalk.
He is dressed in his uniform and cap and is carrying
a sign rolled up and tied. It is cloth.*)

REUBEN. Some promises are hard to keep. Losing Jinny
was like waking up and discovering the sun had a hole in
it. She had the softest black skin I'd ever seen, came out
of her mother like an explosion, and a way of smiling at
you, made you feel somebody had given you a gift. She
was an extension of me! I wanted to see her grown—
bring a boy around here for me to meet—do something—
be something! 12 years old ain't nothin'! It took me 15
years to get seniority on my job—20—30—years to
grow up! 12 years ain't nothin'! (*Confused.*) I promised
her life! We all did—or at least a chance! And right
here! Not out on Route 452! Here, where her memory
is. (*Slight pause.*) But I made Rachel a promise, too. I
couldn't break it—and God knows I wanna' beat
somebody up! (*Slight pause.*) So instead, I went
downtown this morning, and had this sign made to hang
over our porch. Get these folks off their asses. It sure
can't hurt nobody. Not the way I could. But maybe it'll
make somebody come forward.

(REUBEN *crosses* s.r. *on sidewalk and onto the porch.
He enters the house as the lights begin to fade. A*

sign is projected on the screen: "THE KILLERS OF OUR DAUGHTER JINNY ARE FREE ON THE STREETS BECAUSE OUR NEIGHBORS WILL NOT IDENTIFY THEM." Light bathes the sign for one bright moment. Then slowly the sign fades. A larger sign is then projected, an enlargement of the first sign. The stage goes to black as the sign remains projected through the intermission.)

END OF THE FIRST ACT

ACT TWO

Scene 1

(As before. A window in the Tate home is broken, and has been covered over with a piece of cardboard. There is a wreath on the front door. Lights build around the sidewalk. RACHEL *enters* S.L. *She looks tired, drawn, but she has changed into another blouse, skirt and shoes. She is now carrying a bag of groceries. She looks at the sign for a moment, then faces the audience.)*

RACHEL. What is it about men, that won't let them leave well-enough alone? No-one buried in a grave-yard can read the inscription on their headstone! And this neighborhood is dead! (*She is quiet, remembering.*) Reuben had quit prize fighting a year, before they hired him at the bus company. I was three months pregnant with Victor, and we went to Emmett and borrowed seven hundred dollars to make settlement on that house. Place only cost us seven—five, but in those days that was a lot of money! (*Smiles.*) We didn't have a stick of furniture—Reuben never made no money in the ring. Reuben's mother—God rest her soul, gave us all she could, in a card table and two of those fold-up chairs. We ate off that until we bought our first kitchen set—and had to use an old single bed for a couch. (*Slight pause.*) This neighborhood was already black then and we never turned on ourselves—we kept the block clean, swept the sidewalks, gave our little block parties and watched out for each otha's kids. I could run to the store and leave my front door open. (*Pause.*) But I can remember the day, and the hour, that fool down at the end of the street, Julius Williams, began fixing used-cars in the middle of the damn sidewalk, and the oil stains and dirt tracked their way through the entire block. And outside of Reuben and Mr. Neal up at the corner nobody around here said or did anything! Couple months later they shot Scherr in the grocery store — the Armstead family across the street staged a gun-battle with the cops, then the riots closed all the stores on the Avenue, and gave the nighttime to the thieves! It's been like livin' on a burning fuse! (*Quietly.*) Reuben can hang up all the signs he wants to — you can't bring the dead back to life. Not them — not Jinny. I just want to move. (*Crosses onto the porch as the music from the stereo rises and the scrim and dovatien open.*)

(VICTOR *and* RUSSELL *are in the living-room. They are listening to music and watching a portable TV with the sound turned off.* VICTOR *is sitting in the arm chair which has been turned to face the TV.* RUSSELL *sprawls on the sofa.*)

RUSSELL. I wouldn't do it, Vic. You got your whole life ahead of you, Cutty! How you gonna' make it to the Pros if the cops lock you in the 'slams'? (RACHEL *enters the living-room.* RUSSELL *sits up straight on the sofa.*) Hello, Mrs. Tate.

RACHEL. Hello, Russell. (*Closes front door.*) Victor turn that music down, please! (*She passes through the room and exits on the* R., *as* VICTOR *turns the music down grumbling.*)

VICTOR. I can't even hear it! (*Once he feels she is out of earshot, he turns the music up a trifle and sits back down.*)

RUSSELL. Homicide is a deep offense, Vic. And you know if you go to jail, they hafta' send you to Trayburg, and I heard they like to make girls outta' young guys like us. (VICTOR *waves disdainfully*.) What could you do, if two-three old heads—say, dudes in their 20's and 30's jumped your ass and take it?

VICTOR. I'd kill somebody—or kill myself.

RUSSELL. Let the cops catch Zoo and those guys, man! Besides, you don't know that it's Zoo anyway—the rumor is that it was just some *guys* from the Bottom.

VICTOR. If he's the 'runner', I want him to know I'm after him too—maybe he'll give up the dudes that did it.

RUSSELL. (*Amused*.) Paint a sign like your old man did! (*Stands, crosses* S.R. *around sofa*.) Hang it at the bottom of that one. (*Across the air in front of him*.) "Zooman! I'm comin' to get you and your boys!" (*Laughs. Crosses* U.L. *of sofa*.) I'm sorry, Vic, but I never heard of anybody hanging up a sign like that before—the whole neighborhood is laughing—I saw a guy walk by it and fall out on the street, he was laughing so hard! (*Teasing. Crosses to* VICTOR, *spars a few punches to him*.) Did all those fights shake your ole' man's thing loose?

VICTOR. It ain't funny, man—my father has his way—I have mine!

RUSSELL. What if Zoo and them kill you?

VICTOR. They'll just have to kill me, then, OK?

RUSSELL. (*Annoyed*.) Don't play no martyr, Vic—you gettin' like your fatha'! My Mom said, half these niggahs 'round here can't even read that sign, and those that can, it just pisses them off, 'cause it brings the whole neighborhood down—'n somebody's always claimin' our people ain't no good. (*Crosses to* D.L. *of sofa.*) And even if you saw what happened, don't nobody like to deal with the cops. So she don't see why your father put it up in the first place, unless he's just trying to call attention to himself, like you tryin' to do.

VICTOR. (*Rises, crosses to* RUSSELL.) You better stop making fun of my father, Russell — unless you want to fight. (*He turns the TV off.*)

RUSSELL. I didn't say nothin' 'bout your ole' man — I told you what my Mom said. Mr. Williams said it too! (*Pause.*) Hey, I'm trying to save your life, Cutty! Because, I'm not gonna' help you kill nobody — (*Sits on the sofa.*) Zooman or anybody else!

VICTOR. (*Surprised. Crosses to* RUSSELL.) You're not getting the bullets from Ward?

RUSSELL. Nope! They sell bullets in the hardware store, my man — Sears! In fact, I'm sorry I gave you the gun!

VICTOR. You're not getting it back.

RUSSELL. It's not worth a fight, Vic — just leave me out of it.

VICTOR. You're out of it.

RACHEL. (*Offstage; at once.*) Victor?

VICTOR. Huh?

RACHEL. Is your father upstairs?

ASH. (*Emerging at the head of the stair; overlapping to* VICTOR.) Is that your mother?

(*A woman* RACHEL'S *age,* GRACE GEORGES, *enters* S.R. *and crosses to the porch. She will look at the sign, read it for a moment, then shake her head before crossing the porch to the door.*)

VICTOR. (*To* ASH.) She's looking for my father.

(*Loud; crosses* u.s. *to foot of stairs.*) He went to Buster's Bar—him and Uncle Emmett! Said he'd be right back.

RACHEL. (*Still offstage.*) Where'd this potato salad come from?

ASH. (*Starting down.*) That man Jackson—said his wife made some more—just in case. It's the second batch he's brought over here. He came while you were at the store. He acts funny to me! (GRACE *rings the doorbell;* ASH *looks toward the door.*) Who is this?

RACHEL. (*Offstage.*) You're too suspicious Ash.

ASH. (*Moving toward door.*) I think that Jackson knows something about the shooting. (*Doorbell rings again.*)

GRACE. (*Outside at once.*) Rachel. It's me honey, Grace!

RACHEL. (*Offstage.*) Let her in!

ASH. (*Crosses to front door, opens.* VICTOR *crosses* s.l. *to stereo.* ASH, *simultaneously with* RACHEL *above.*) Hello!

RUSSELL. (*Rises. Crosses* u.s.l. *to* VICTOR.) I gotta' go Cutty—my Mom wants to know when the Wake is. (GRACE *steps inside smiling at* ASH.)

GRACE. (*Overlapping.*) I'm Grace Georges, a friend of Rachel's from down the street? (ASH *gestures for* GRACE *to enter. They cross to* u.c. *of sofa.*)

VICTOR. Tuesday—Lincoln Funeral Home.

RUSSELL. (*Starting out.*) You're wrong, Vic.

VICTOR. She wasn' your sista'.

GRACE. Hi, Russell.

RUSSELL. Hello Mrs. Georges. (RUSSELL *and* VICTOR *move toward the door.*) See you later, Vic. (RUSSELL *exits front door, crosses off porch and exits* s.r..)

ASH. Have a seat, hon, she'll be out in a minute—I'm

her Cousin, Ash Boswell. (ASH *and* GRACE *shake hands.*)

GRACE. Pleased to meet you. Hi, Victor.

VICTOR. (*Closes door and starts to dining-room.*) Hello.

GRACE. I'm sorry about your sister.

(RACHEL *enters* U.R. *as* VICTOR *smiles faintly at* GRACE, *passing his mother on his way offstage.* RACHEL *seems a little tired.*)

VICTOR. I'ma get something to eat. (*Exits.*)

RACHEL. (*Nods.*) Hi Grace.

GRACE. How you feelin' girl? (RACHEL *crosses to* GRACE, *who takes her hand comfortingly.*) I just dropped by to pay my respects. Denise started to come over, but she's feeling a bit under the weather — asthma's bothering her in this heat, chile. (GRACE *sits* L. *sofa.*) Mike said he'd see Reuben at the Layout — he's got to work. (RACHEL *goes to the stereo and turns it off.*)

ASH. (*To* GRACE.) Can I get you a little plate of something? We've got plenty of potato salad, and I'm fixing some greens — and chicken — and cornbread.

GRACE. Nawww — nope, I'd better not. Mike'll be home soon and if I eat over here, I sure won't feel like standin' in front of no hot stove cooking his dinner — No, thank you. Girl, the way that man loves to eat, he'd have a shit fit! I'm not going to stay that long. (ASH *shrugs.*) Girl, I guess you've just about run outta' line, huh? (RACHEL *nods.*) It's a shame, Rachel. I think I woulda went out of my mind if it hada' been Denise — I don't know how you can stand it. Theyda' had to carry me to the hospital — somethin'! My only child? Theyda' had to strap me down! (*Pause.*) I am really sorry it happened Rachel. If you need anything, just send Victor—or anybody!

RACHEL. Thanks, Grace—Ash came to help me out.

GRACE. (*To* ASH.) My little girl, Denise and Jinny useta' play together. Rachel is strong—if it hada' been Denise—and the way Mike loves that child? They mighta' had to strap us both down! Men always love their little girls the most. (*There is an awkward moment of silence.*) Well, I didn't intend to stay long. (GRACE *starts to rise.*)

RACHEL. You don't have to rush, Grace. (GRACE *sits.*)

GRACE. I didn't lock my front door, Girl—but I did want to ask you one thing. (*Lower.*) Why did you let Reuben hang that sign up, Rachel? He's got these people around here climbing the walls! Don't none of them appreciate it—in fact, Cortez and Williams told Mike they were planning to hold a block meeting about it. (*Pause.*) And the truth is, I kinda' think it makes the whole street look bad myself. You know what I mean? Like, what if you didn't see it? Thing like that lumps the good with the bad—and everytime you turn around black folks are saying something terrible about each other! "We can't get together—our men ain't no good—we're triflin', everywhere we live is a slum!" I get tired of it myself—and Reuben's sign makes this look like the worse place in the world.

ASH. (*Crosses; sits on window seat.*) But then you didn't lose your little Denise, did you Honey?

GRACE. If we had, I wouldn't have let Mike advertise about it! That's y'all's private business!

ASH. Seems like a killing on the block would be everybody's business . . .

GRACE. The Tates ain't no better than nobody else!

Rachel and Reuben didn't come to Myrtle Coleman's layout — or to Mr. Stewart's funeral either! I didn't see the Tates get excited when those hoodlums raped Lou Jefferson's little girl — or robbed my place! Why should anybody go out of their way for them? I didn't hang up no sign!

RACHEL. Did you see it Grace?

GRACE. (*Stiffens defensively.*) What? No! Don't you accuse me!

(*Two bricks crash against the screen door, break and splatter. A bottle breaks beside them. GRACE screams at the crash. At once, VICTOR enters suddenly and crosses the room quickly to the front door. ASH stands and crosses U.C. of sofa. GRACE stands and crosses L. of sofa. RACHEL stands and crosses D.L.*)

VICTOR. (*Incredulous.*) They trying to knock the door down! (*Moves to the door. ASH follows him.*)

ASH. Stay in here, Boy! (VICTOR *is outside, where he pulls the gun. ASH sees him, RACHEL cannot.*)

GRACE. (*Interjecting.*) I knew this would happen!

ASH. What are you doing with that Victor? (ASH *crosses onto porch.*) He's got a gun. (VICTOR *crosses off porch to* D.R. *sidewalk.*)

RACHEL. What gun? (*Crosses below sofa to front door.*) Victor?

ASH. (*Overlapping.*) Git in here! (*Tosses bricks and kicks glass off porch.*)

VICTOR. No.

RACHEL. (*Reaches door.*) Give me that thing!

VICTOR. Suppose they come through here again? What do we do then? We need protection Mom! The Tates just don't let people mess with them!

RACHEL. (*Steps onto the porch and crosses to* VIC-TOR.) You give me that damn gun right now! (*She snatches at it.*) You give it to me! You hear me? (*She swings at him and snatches it.*) Damn you Victor! Are we supposed to lose you, too? (VICTOR *is immediately sorry, as* RACHEL *looks at the gun with a mixture of horror and rage.*)

ASH. (*Quickly.*) Boy, get in here and get a broom and clean this mess up off the porch!

RACHEL. (VICTOR *starts past* RACHEL *and she lashes out, hitting him, in tears.*) Don't you eva'! (VICTOR *moves past her quickly.*) I'll knock the living hell outta' you! You hear me, Victor?

VICTOR. Yes. (VICTOR *exits offstage, as* ASH *holds the door for* RACHEL *as she enters. She hands the gun to* ASH.)

RACHEL. Throw this thing in the trash.

ASH. Where in the name of hell did he get it?

GRACE. It's goin' to get worse, Rachel. People don't like being accused when they haven't done anything!

RACHEL. Get the hell out of here, Grace—Get out! (GRACE, *angry, starts out without a word. She goes to the door, stops for a moment to look at* ASH *and* RACHEL, *then exits. In the house, there is a moment of quiet.*)

RACHEL. (*Paces* S.L.) Glass all over the porch! Did you hear him—The Tates! Will somebody please tell me what good that sign is accomplishing? Are we supposed to take turns sitting guard on the front steps? We're supposed to be in mourning for our daughter—there's a wreath on the door, and where the hell is he? Comes back three days, disrupts everything—turns things inside out. Putting up signs, it's—it's disrespectful! (*To herself.*) I almost wish I had let him beat up a few of them.

ASH. No you don't.

RACHEL. I don't want this! (*VICTOR re-enters with a broom and dustpan and crosses to the front door. ASH crosses to front door.*) I'm sick of you Victor — give me that broom and go someplace outta' my sight! (*She snatches the broom, and starts outside. VICTOR starts back in, and heads upstairs.*)

ASH. Are you all right?

RACHEL. (*Outside sweeping.*) I'm fine! Just fine! (*ASH starts toward the dining-room looking at the gun and shaking her head. RACHEL, sweeps glass D.S. on porch; to herself.*) I didn't go to Mr. Stewart's funeral because Reuben wasn't here! And he wasn't here when the Jefferson girl got raped — and I get tired of walking around by myself or with my kids, Reuben! Florence wasn't the first one! (*She bends over and picks up the debris.*) What kinda people would do something like this? (*She starts in, leaving the broom behind.*)

(*From the S.L. REUBEN and EMMETT emerge. It is clear they have been in a fight. They both seem in pain, EMMETT holding his arm, REUBEN's hand is wrapped in a handkerchief. They cross R. on sidewalk to porch . . . They both have trouble making it up to the porch. However, once REUBEN sees the debris his own pain is unimportant. Carrying the broom, he reaches for the door and enters, leaving EMMETT behind him.*)

REUBEN. Rachel? What the hell happened?

RACHEL. (*Re-enters, carrying dustpan, sees him and is shocked.*) Oh, my God! (*Crosses S.L. of arm chair. EMMETT enters.*)

REUBEN. (*Quickly.*) I'm all right. We got into a fight at Buster's — what happened?

ASH. (*Re-entering; takes broom from Reuben.*) Some fools threw a couple bricks at the door — (RACHEL *leads* REUBEN *to the sofa.*) Probably some nasty kids — (*Sees* EMMETT.) what happened to you two?

RACHEL. A fight at Buster's! (ASH *exits* U.R. *with broom.*)

EMMETT. We turned that Bar, OUT! (*Staggers in and flops into window seat.*) Didn't we Reub? (ASH *re-enters and crosses to* EMMETT.)

RACHEL. Did you have to get into a fight? (RACHEL *places dustpan on floor near arm chair.*)

REUBEN. (*Crosses* D.S. *of sofa.*) What choice did I have?

EMMETT. (*Overlapping.*) We didn't have no choice, Rachel! (*Aside.*) Pure case of survival.

ASH. (*Quickly; closing window.*) You half drunk! (EMMETT *makes a face at her.*)

REUBEN. We were drinking two beers — and this fella' from Croskey Street — I've seen him before. He walks up in *my* face, and tells *me*, he didn't want us in there — unless I took my sign down! (*Mimics.*) "You givin' the black community a bad name!" Here's a man, in my face, for no reason, and I'm givin' the community a bad name? (*Quieter.*) I tol' him, I wasn't takin' nothin' down, until it got some results! (*Sits on sofa.*)

EMMETT. Then the other guy punched me — and Reub punched him, and it was on! (VICTOR *emerges; crosses down steps stands* U.C.)

ASH. (*Crosses* D.S. *of* EMMETT, *examines his arm.*) Hold still and let me look at this arm, fool!

REUBEN. (*Overlapping.*) Help me get this jacket off Honey? (RACHEL *crosses to* REUBEN, *stands* U.S. *of sofa. Helps* REUBEN *take off jacket reluctantly; lays jacket over back of sofa.*)

VICTOR. What's going on? (*Crosses* U.R. *of sofa.*)

EMMETT. Hey, Nephew—me and your fatha' was in a fight! You shoulda' seen him . . . He's still got a mean left hook!

RACHEL. You know how crazy you sound? (*Crosses* L. *of sofa.*) Two grown men bragging?

REUBEN. Who's bragging? We didn't start it!

RACHEL. Is that where Victor got it—

REUBEN. What'd you expect me to do, Rachel?!

RACHEL. —pointing a gun all over the porch.

REUBEN. What?!—A gun! (*Rises.*)

RACHEL. A gun, that's what!

REUBEN. (*Crosses around sofa to* VICTOR. VICTOR *backs* U.S. *to foot of stairs.*) What were you doing with a gun, Victor—where'd you get it?!

RACHEL. (*Crosses to* U.R. *of sofa.*) Why weren't you here to find out?!

VICTOR. I found it.

REUBEN. Where?!

VICTOR. It wasn't loaded!

RACHEL. (*Crosses* D.L.) You had no business with it!

REUBEN. You want me to let loose on you, boy? (*The phone interrupts as* ASH *also chimes in.*)

ASH. This arm feels broken to me.

EMMETT. I been workin' in hospitals all my life! If it was broken, I'd know if it was broke!—

ASH. (*Exploiting the occasion to rescue* VICTOR; *To* EMMETT.) Come on you ole' fool and let me see if I can do anything with this. (ASH *helps* EMMETT *stand. They cross* U.C.) You ain't got the sense you was born with. Like I said, you Tates is one evil bunch when you drink. (*To* VICTOR.) Come on and help me, boy! (VICTOR *rushes to obey. They exit as* REUBEN *goes to answer the insistent phone.*)

REUBEN. Hello? Yes this is Reuben Tate . . . Say that

to my face, punk! Come around here and say that to my face! (*He slams the phone down.*)

RACHEL. So now you're inviting them! (*Crosses and sits* D.L. *chair.*)

REUBEN. Rachel, I'm not going to stand around while people beat us the hell up! (*The phone interrupts again. This time,* REUBEN *rushes to grab it.*) Listen here, you—?? What? Channel 22? Yes, this is the Tate's residence. You're talking to him. Channel 22? Well, I hung it the other day. But I've never been on TV before, what would I say? Unhuh—just talk about the sign? Guess so—can't hurt. Unhuh. Well, I'd have to think about it—give me a day—I'll let you know. Sure, thanks for calling. (*He hangs up. Crosses* D.S. *to* L. *of sofa.*) They heard about the sign and want to interview me.

RACHEL. I'm sick of that sign!

REUBEN. What's wrong with the sign?

RACHEL. We're supposed to be in mourning—We lost Jinny three days ago—why are you doing this now?

REUBEN. (*Crosses to* RACHEL.) Rachel_ that sign hasn't hurt anybody unless they feel guilty—it doesn't fire bullets—punch-out people—

RACHEL. It is making people hate us, Reuben!

REUBEN. (*Angrily.*) That's because there's not *enough* signs! I'ma put up more of 'em—(*Crosses* D.R.C.) saturate the whole neighborhood! Telephone poles—store windows—busses—let everybody know! They want to be nasty?

RACHEL. You're making this a side-show! You know that?

REUBEN. The side-show was the day they ran through here, shot up the street, killed our daughter, and nobody on this block did anything about it! (*Crosses* D.R. *of sofa.*) I'm not gonna' let them forget Jinny's life!

RACHEL. Jinny? Who the hell is that? Guns, fights, signs on telephone poles—(*Rises, crosses to sofa.*) TV interviews and all in the name of Jinny? Hallelujah! Well *Jinny* was gentle, Reuben—did you forget that? A shy child—and this is her time! The last little bit of her time we have left, and someone in this family better pay her some attention, you know that? Somebody better pay some attention to her!

(REUBEN *turns; faces* RACHEL. REUBEN *starts to reply, but is interrupted by the reappearance of* ASH, EMMETT *and* VICTOR. *They enter urgently,* EMMETT *obviously in deep pain, bent over holding his bruised arm which has been wrapped in an improvised sling bandage.* ASH *crosses* U.C. *of sofa.* EMMETT *assisted by* VICTOR, *crosses to front door, crosses onto porch and exits* S.R.)

ASH. Come on, Reuben, we gotta' drive him to the hospital. He's getting worse. I know his arm is broken. (ASH *picks up* REUBEN'S *jacket,* REUBEN *takes jacket and crosses to front door. Exits* S.R., *following* VICTOR *and* EMMETT. ASH *crosses to front door, exits closing front door, crosses off porch; exits* S.R. RACHEL *is left alone.*)

RACHEL. (*Quietly to no one in particular.*) Somebody needs to pay more attention to Jinny.

(*Lights fade out and rise up on* ZOOMAN *once more at the platform.*)

ZOOMAN. It kin be fun being on the run. One time me an' Stockholm dodged the big blue fools for ten days. We holed up in a 'junkie-hole' right 'round the corner

from where we robbed the dude! Night-time, we useta'
go out, ride the bus crosstown, break into a store or
somethin', then get on the same bus and come back.
Like Robin Hood! Sometime we just laid-dead and got
high—Christine would sneak in with chicken and shit
from Kentucky-fried. (*Pause.*) I been goin' with
Christine almost two years—she ain't got no kids of
mine yet, but she says she wants one—But Christine
can't half take care of the kid Arnold gave her—little
mothafucka' be dirty all the time, smellin' like pee, and
Christine be layin' up on the bed watchin' television—besides, she ain't got as much education as I got!
(*Slight pause. Crosses to* s.r. *sidewalk.*) I ain't really
worried yet. And I happen to know, if a black kills a
black, and they don't catch you right away, they liable
to forget about it—But that niggah with them signs?
Ain't nobody ever pulled that kinda shit before! Kill-
ings, rapes, drugs—all kinds of shit be goin' on everyday
and nobody says nothin'! That section was always run-
down and dangerous—Vacant 'junkie-holes' everywhea',
trash on the streets—(*Shakes head.*) Always some
mothafucka' wanna' be a hero! (*Crosses* s.r. *to platform.*) Wasn' neva' no stores on the Avenue! You have
to go half way around the world to get to the Chinese
laundry—get your clothes cleaned, or your shoes fixed!
Ain' nothin' in there but barber shops and junky corner-
groceries—and every now and then a drug-store where
the man sells you your pills and cough-syrup behind a
bullet-proof glass! Shiiittt! The first junkie I ever met
was a mothafucka' lived 'cross the street—and I know
every mothafucka' that's stealin', muggin', hustlin', and
procurin'—grew up with all of 'em! (*Crosses to* s.l.
sidewalk.) Everybody I know buys hot clothes! Curtis'
mother? Walkin' around passin' out all that, Let-Jesus-

Save-You-shit? Buys truckloads of hot dresses and be sellin' them to her Holy-Moly congregation. And I've seen Greenie's fatha' stealin' cookies out the supermarket — puttin' tuna fish and shit under his coat. (*Crosses to platform.*) Now he's gonna make that zoo a neighborhood puttin' everybody on me? The little bitch was in the way, that's all! Who the fuck he think he is? Sendin' people afta' me, like I'm some animal! If he wants to blame somebody — you don't leave no little girl sittin' on her steps by herself nowadays! I don't let my sista' go out by herself. He shoulda' known better — what kinda' fatha' is he? (*Slight pause.*) But I'll tell you what — if somebody don't git his ass straight soon, I'ma show him just what a killer is — Niggahs can't be heroes, don't he know nothin'?

(ZOOMAN'S *music comes up for a moment, then begins to fade as the light around him goes to black. Simultaneously the light builds around the Tate household.* EMMETT'S *arm is in a sling and cast. They are all dressed in black. It is evening.*)

ASH. How was the service?

REUBEN. Not much you can say about a Wake, Ash. They said the prayers, blessed the casket — one little girl got up and read a little poem from her school, but there's not that much to say about a Wake.

EMMETT. What was that preacher's name, Reub?

REUBEN. Walker — Rev. Walker.

EMMETT. (*To* ASH.) He gave a good eulogy. It made me feel better — he didn' have the whole place cryin'! (RACHEL *sobs.*)

VICTOR. (*At once.*) You all right, Mom? (*She nods.*)

EMMETT. Like the way he talked about kids — and heaven, you didn't feel weighted down.

RACHEL. (*Overlapping.*) I'm just numb, son. (*Slight pause.*)

EMMETT. At least it felt that way to me.

REUBEN. (*To* ASH.) Your old girlfriend Mrs. Rheinhard was there. She asked about you.

ASH. Really? That was nice of her—how'd she look? The last time I talked to her, she was complaining about her arthritis.

REUBEN. She looked all right to me.

EMMETT. (*Out of nowhere, as* VICTOR *opens* S.R. *window.*) Children must be spared hell's fire, 'cause they're innocent. You hear that Reub?

REUBEN. (*Nods.*) A couple of the drivers I work with were there—and Lefty Cohen my old trainer—did you see him? (RACHEL *slams register closed.*) Rachel? Honey, you want an aspirin? (RACHEL *shakes her head 'no'.*)

ASH. Did they sing? (*Crosses* S.R. *around sofa; sits* S.R. *side of sofa.*)

EMMETT. Nearer My God To Thee—all the standard stuff. (*To* REUBEN.) What was that one Jinny liked so much?

REUBEN and ASH. Amazing Grace.

EMMETT. They sung that. It was a nice service, I thought. (*Looks around.*) Jinny looked peaceful.

REUBEN. I was just thinking about her—she'd be sleeping by now—only child I ever saw slept with a smile on her face.

VICTOR. Didn't look nothin' like her to me. Why'd they put all that powder on her face?

REUBEN. That's just how they do it, son.

RACHEL. Other Undertakers don't make people look like that, and you know it! I've been to enough Wakes—(*Almost crying.*) and the people didn't look like that!

REUBEN. What can we do about it now—take her someplace else?

RACHEL. That's not funny!

REUBEN. (*Gentle.*) I didn't like it anymore than you did.

RACHEL. The whole thing was just so ugly! (REUBEN *puts his arm around her.*)

ASH. Y'all got to forgive me for not going—I started to after you left, but I couldn't. I didn't want to see her like that. I sat here trying to find something to do—I even laid down to rest, and was surprised when the doorbell woke me up, that I had fallen asleep. I dreamed about her. She was standing there, by the window, smiling. It startled me, it seemed so real.

EMMETT. We understand. (*To* REUBEN.) Who sent that big wreath? The one with 12 carnations on it?

REUBEN. I think her class took up a collection—I was surprised to see a bouquet from the block committee. Ash? Who came to the door—you said somebody woke you up?

ASH. That man who's been bringing all that potato-salad over here—Jackson. This time he brought a pot of greens—said he wanted to talk to you and Rachel. He acts funny to me.

REUBEN. What did he do?

ASH. Nothin'—I don't know—he just acts funny—like he wants to say something and never says it! He's been back and forth over here everyday—he acts like he's got things botherin' him. When I asked him to come in, he almost ran off the porch.

EMMETT. Maybe he saw something, Reub.

REUBEN. Jackson was at work.

EMMETT. Maybe his wife saw something—she's the one makin' all the food—and he keeps comin' by to see if anybody else came forward. You know we don't like to stick our necks out — and he acted strange to me, the first time he came by.

REUBEN. She does have a clear view of the street from her yard — maybe she did see it. She could be scared. They both might be.

EMMETT. They probably trying to get out of it!

ASH. He said he'd be by later.

REUBEN. (*To* EMMETT.) Everybody ain't like that! A whole lot of them came to the Wake.

RACHEL. Well, which ones raised all the hell, Reuben?

REUBEN. Those people were ignorant — Smith, Williams and Judson wasn' never worth a damn!

EMMETT. (*Overlapping.*) Anybody want a beer? (*Rises.*) Reub?

RACHEL. (*As* EMMETT *rises.*) They whispered about his sign all through the whole damn service.

ASH. (*At once.*) You don't need no more to drink, Mistah. (EMMETT *waves at her disdainfully as he exits* U.R.)

RACHEL. (*To* ASH.) They wrote threats — and, and filth in the Register! (*She holds up the book.*) The only thing we got left! The layout register! You ever in your life hear of anything as rotten and lowdown as that? (*She throws it down.*)

REUBEN. You know some kids wrote that — look at the handwriting! (*Rises, crosses around sofa.*) A lot of people came over to me and said they were glad about the sign —

RACHEL. Is Davis a kid? (*To* VICTOR.) Tell your father what he told you —

VICTOR. He just said he was sorry about Jinny, and he thought the sign would bring us trouble.

REUBEN. I didn't hear him say that. (EMMETT *enters with beer, crosses* U.C. *of sofa.*)

VICTOR. He was in line — he leaned over and

whispered it to me. Uncle Emmett heard it. (EMMETT *hands* REUBEN *a beer.*)

EMMETT. Yeah, I heard it. (*Crosses* S.R. *to* VICTOR.) I tried to tap him with this cast a couple times, too!

RACHEL. Did you hear Julius Williams shouting all over the sidewalk?

REUBEN. (*Crosses* U.S. *of arm chair.*) Julius Williams ain't gonna' do a damn thing—he is nothin' but mouth. If he ever lights a cigarette in front of this house, I'll have him locked up!

RACHEL. And if someone else decides to set fire to it?

ASH. Fire?

RACHEL. They were threatening to burn the damn place down!

REUBEN. Then let 'em! I'm not taking down that sign because some drunken bum like Williams got loud! (*JACKSON enters* D.R. *with two loaves of bread; crosses onto porch, stopping to look at the sign.*)

EMMETT. Reub, I think I know how you feel, but people ain't like they used to be, they do vicious things nowadays Reub. You got this to protect. (*The doorbell rings.* ASH *rises; crosses to front door.* RACHEL *rises and places register on chair; crosses to stereo, tosses glove and exits* U.R.)

REUBEN. That sign doesn't come down until someone comes forward.

ASH. (*Opens the door.*) Mr. Jackson! (*Everyone turns around.* REUBEN *rises and goes to the door.* EMMETT *crosses and sits* S.L. *sofa.*)

REUBEN. Jackson, come on in! (*JACKSON crosses through the doorway.*)

JACKSON. No thanks, I'm on my way to work. I just came by to bring this bread my wife made. (*He hands it to* ASH *as* REUBEN *approaches.* ASH *exits* U.R. *with bread*.) She said she knew y'all would be havin' company and we both—me and my wife figured Rachel would have enough to do.

REUBEN. Thanks.

JACKSON. (ASH *re-enters and crosses* U.L. *of sofa*.) I came by earlier—how's your Missus?

REUBEN. OK. (*There's a slight awkward silence;* JACKSON *is uneasy*.) Jackson—your wife? She saw the whole thing, didn't she?

JACKSON. (*Surprised and hurt*.) No, Reuben!

ASH. (*Crosses* U.L. *of arm chair*.) Ask him why he's been comin' over here so much then?

JACKSON. (*To* ASH *and* REUBEN.) My wife and me thought y'all needed a little help—I—My wife's been after me to tell y'all how we felt about you and the little girl. I came and took Rachel to the hospital when she was born. I—but I just couldn't say it. I tol' my wife, I said, "Saying' something like that to people can embarrass a man!" But I figured if I brought something ova'—a little gift or something, I wouldn't have to say it, 'cause y'all would know. But she kept pesterin' me—"You ain't said it!" She said that everyday—and it was on me, 'cause I took her to the hospital.

REUBEN. Jackson, I—

JACKSON. Let me say it, all right? We like y'all! You and Rachel raised nice kids, and y'all ain't loud and don't raise a whole lotta' hell around here! And I'm glad you put up that sign, but we didn't see nothin'—my wife or me. (*Indignant*.) We ain't them kinda' people Reuben! (*Slight pause*. RACHEL *re-enters; stands* U.C. *in hall unseen by* JACKSON.) They come by my house this evenin' to ask me, if me and my wife would join some march they plannin'. A group of 'em intend to pull that sign down, or set it on fire. I don't want no part of it!

But we—(*Pause. Crosses to door.*) It's getting kinda' late, and I gotta' go to work. Tell your Missus that bread's an easy recipe. My wife said, if she wants it, she'll give it to her. (JACKSON *turns away and starts out.*) Goodnight. (JACKSON *exits through front door; crosses off porch and exits* D.R.)

REUBEN. (REUBEN *crosses onto porch.*) I'm sorry, Jackson. (JACKSON *doesn't hear.* REUBEN *re-enters.* RACHEL *crosses to foot of stairs. The family is quiet for a while.* REUBEN *closes the door and crosses to* S.R. *window.*)

EMMETT. Everybody makes mistakes.

RACHEL. That sign is making us crazy!

REUBEN. (*Irritated.*) The sign stays up. (*Crosses* D.R. *of sofa.*)

ASH. I think it's too dangerous to keep up now, Reuben. Why not take it down just for tonight? After all, you can always put it back up.

EMMETT. After the funeral wouldn't hurt. (REUBEN *shakes his head 'no'. The phone rings almost like a reprise.* VICTOR *rises to get it.*)

REUBEN. Once she's in the ground, they'll forget it.

VICTOR. Hello? Who? (*To* REUBEN.) It's for you. (REUBEN *crosses to* VICTOR, *takes receiver.* VICTOR *crosses* S.L. *and picks up and reads the register.*) And if they ever catch the boys, these people won't even remember her name! Besides, it's the principle of the thing. (ASH *sits in the arm chair.* REUBEN *puts receiver to ear.*) Hello? Who? Sergeant Harrison? No, I'm all right, we're not long back from the layout, so we are a little tired. Unhuh—you caught one of them. (RACHEL *crosses, sits* S.R. *sofa.*)

ASH. Thank God!

REUBEN. Unhuh—well, that's a start. I hope so— (*Smiles suddenly.*) You saw the picture in the paper? Yeah, I useta' box light-heavy, I was ranked number three for a while. Well, they're supposed to send some people out to interview me. (*Chuckles.*) Listen, you open up us bus-drivers anything's liable to come out. Unhuh. (*Serious.*) There is one thing, though. Could you have a patrol-car pass through this street from time to time tonight? No—nothing serious—fine. Thanks, Sarge. You too! (*Hangs up. Crosses* U.R. *of sofa.*) A patrol-car will swing through here tonight, are y'all satisfied?

EMMETT. When you ever known the police to be where they're supposed to be, when they're supposed to be there? Man you crazy! I know what I'ma do, and it ain't gonna' wait on no cops eitha'!

ASH. (*Giving* EMMETT *a nasty look.*) What did he say about the boys?

REUBEN. (*Sitting.*) They caught one of 'em. He's fifteen.

ASH. They get younger and weaker in every generation.

REUBEN. (*Disturbed.*) There were two of 'em. They picked up some kid named Stockholm and he told on the other one—boy they call Zooman. (*To himself.*) I never thought of them as that young. They felt like men.

RACHEL. I'm glad they caught him. (*Rises, crosses to* S.R. *window.*)

EMMETT. (*Overlapping.*) They got 'em out here sellin' dope at 10 and 11—where have you been, Reub?

REUBEN. (*Crosses* L. *towards* VICTOR.) You ever heard of them, Victor?

RACHEL. How would Victor know somebody named Zooman?

VICTOR. I've heard of him—I don't know him.

RACHEL. You better not know him!

REUBEN. Is that the one you wanted to get? (VICTOR *nods.*) Did you know he had done it?

VICTOR. Nawww—it was the rumor that it came from

down the Bottom and he's the 'runner' down there—(*Shrugs.*) So—

RACHEL. (*Crosses to* R. *of sofa.*) What? What kinda crazy—are you in some gang?

VICTOR. No! That was just the rumor on the street—I'm not in no gang! (*A long pause.*) Can I sit outside on the steps?

REUBEN. Go 'head. (VICTOR *places register in* S.L. *chair and crosses* U.S. *of sofa to front door, crosses onto porch and sits on steps.* RACHEL *crosses to* S.R. *window, looks out.* REUBEN *crosses* R. *above sofa.*) The kids know who's on the street and who isn't.

RACHEL. (*Calmly.*) Will you please take that sign down?

REUBEN. Nope. The cop just said (*Crosses to* D.R. *'window'*) he thought it was a good idea to leave it up. They got a lotta' phone calls today after my picture was in the paper—said a lot of people are behind it. (RACHEL *shakes her head.*)

ASH. Rachel, you want an aspirin?

RACHEL. (*Crosses to* REUBEN.) I want this man to take down that damn sign!

REUBEN. Rachel, why can't you back me up! When I was hanging those telephone pole signs? (*Crosses to* S.L. *window.*) The Democratic Committeemen over on Shelby Street? Man ain't never spoke to me since we moved here—came up to me and told me I was right! Right! Morgan the barber put one in his shop, and it made him feel proud. Cobb at the corner grocery—Baker at the shoe-shine parlor, they all said they were for it!

RACHEL. (*Crosses* D.C. *to* REUBEN.) You put up a few signs, get your name in the paper and you're Martin Luther King?

REUBEN. (*Turns facing* RACHEL.) Nobody's trying to be King—If somebody comes forward maybe—those boys won't run through here no more!

RACHEL. I thought you put it up for Jinny?

REUBEN. I did!

RACHEL. The people around here, want to do something to you, Reuben.

EMMETT. (*Rises.*) I got to agree with her Reuben—all that stuff you talkin' (*Crosses* U.L. *of sofa.*) Listen, we got to be on guard right here!

REUBEN. Goddamn—don't y'all understand? You can't live across the street from me, see my daughter get killed and not do nothin'! I don't have to be in no newspapers—or TV either! You can't do that shit to me!

RACHEL. (*Crosses to* D.L. *chair and picks up register.*) You know what they wrote in this book? (*Crosses to* L. *of arm chair and shows* ASH *the register.*) They want to kill you Reuben—and I love you!

REUBEN. Then they gonna hafta do it. I'm not scared of them.

RACHEL. You're not scared, but the rest of us are scared to death.

REUBEN. I can't take the sign down, until somebody comes forward—and I don't want anybody in this family to mess with it, eitha'! (*Crosses to* D.R. *window'.*)

RACHEL. (*Crosses to* REUBEN.) We just got through sitting in front of Jinny—and Reuben I don't want to wind up sitting in front of you. (*Hesitant.*) If you don't take it down—I want you to leave! (RACHEL *exits up the stairs. There is silence.* ASH *rises and crosses* U.L., *exits up the stairs. The silence continues.* EMMETT *picks up jacket and exits* U.R. *with can of beer.*)

REUBEN. Rachel? I ain't goin' nowhere! (*Exits* U.R. *as the lights fade and the scrim closes.* VICTOR *rises and crosses* s.l. *on the sidewalk. He is a little sad. Lights rise on the sidewalk.*)

VICTOR. They always tell me, that I've got a better education than they had — that I know more — should do great things, but they never let me say anything. I don't have a voice in nothin' — no opinions, no pros — cons — and most of the time they talk over me like I'm not even there. And I know a whole lot more than they know. (*Pause.*) I'm the one misses Jinny the most — I was around her the most! We useta' have arguments sometimes, but she was all I had — you can't talk to them — not like you can with someone you're close to — grow up with. Me and Jinny had secrets — things they never even knew we talked about. They weren't big secrets, but sometimes she would tell me things — like how she wanted them to get back together. And how angry she would get with my Mom, when she wouldn't let my father stay here. She told me once, that sometimes, when she missed him a lot, she would show-off just to get on my Mom's nerves so bad, she would have to call my father over, just to punish her. At least she would see him. (*Slight pause.*) That's what she was doin' the other day — and they don't know that. I know it, but I'll never tell them! (ZOOMAN *enters* s.r., *crosses to* d.r. *sidewalk.*)

(ZOOMAN *glances at the sign, he notices* VICTOR *who notices him. They both straighten.* ZOOMAN *reaches into his pocket, the one away from the audience, and removes his knife. We hear it click. He holds it down at his side, out of sight.* VICTOR *registers an immediate sense of caution. Both boys are tense as they start toward each other at the same time. They will reach each other and pass by in silence, aware and prepared for one another.* VICTOR *goes directly to the porch, and looks back at* ZOOMAN. ZOOMAN *exits* S.L.; *he re-enters and crosses* S.R. *on the sidewalk to the* S.R. *platform. When he reaches it, he looks at his knife, closes it and puts it back into his pocket. He smiles as* VICTOR *exits through the house.* VICTOR *crosses* U.C. *and exits up the stairs as the lights fade in the house and rise on the sidewalk and* D.R. *platform. Through all of this* ZOOMAN's *music has played.*)

ZOOMAN. They got me a little scared. If they got Stockholm's ass in the slams, it's just a matter of time, 'cause the Big Blues put a lotta' pressure on you once they pick you up. Anybody can snap under that. I'm not even sure what *I* would do! 'Specially since I got a previous record—the Big Blues can be a bitch! At the 7th? They hit my little brother Kenny 'cross the mouth with a blackjack! (*To himself.*) Stockholm probably screamed his guts out. Y'all won't have to wait too long—Stock probably gave the Man a complete description by now. I'm not mad with him, though—his Mom probably got him some wise-ass lawyer and that mothafucka' will make Stockholm swear he wasn' even there! "Zooman had the gun!" "Zooman fired the shots" "Zooman told me to do it!" (*Smiles.*) It's all right, 'cause I'd put the whole thing on him if I got the chance. Don't *nobody* want to go to jail for murder. My Aunt—she'll be down there cryin' all ova' the place. My Mom won't come—and my fatha' probably won't even know about it, unless they put it in the Chicago papers. (*Shakes head.*) That dude—if I had a nickel for everytime I laid eyes on that mothafucka' I wouldn' have fifty-cents! (*Tired.*) Last night, I slept squattin' over the toilet seat in the train station with a faggot!

Mothafucka' had the nerve to proposition me, while I was peein'! I kicked his ass, and when the mothafucka' started pleadin' I jes *cut* the mothafucka'—shiiitt! And y'all got the nerve to hunt me? Y'all let anything walk the streets—and you mothafuckas' never showed me no mercy! (*Pause.*) I'll be off your streets soon, don't worry—I just got one more thing to do.

(ZOOMAN *steps from the platform and starts across the stage boldly toward the* TATE *house. Before he reaches the steps he is hollering, his knife in his hand.*)

ZOOMAN. Hey mothafucka'! This is Zooman out here! (*He reaches up and begins to rip and tear at the sign.*) Don't nobody do this shit! You don't send people after me! You hear that mothafucka'!? This is Zooman you fuckin' with! (*Lights come on inside the house and* EM- METT *half frightened, half asleep comes down the stairs with a gun in his hand.*)

EMMETT. Reuben? Reuben? (EMMETT *crosses* U.C. *of sofa. He fires immediately through the window. The shot hits* ZOOMAN *and knocks him down; and he pulls down the sign with him. He is in surprised agony for a few moments. He staggers and crawls off the porch to* D.C. *on the sidewalk.*) Reuben! They're outside! Reuben!

REUBEN. Emmett—what the hell are you doin'? (*He starts down; crosses to* EMMETT.)

EMMETT. They're outside! They were pulling on the sign! I heard 'em—it woke me up! They were trying to come in! (REUBEN *starts toward the front door and crosses onto the porch.*)

REUBEN. That sounded like some kid—

EMMETT. That wasn' no kid I heard! (REUBEN *crosses* D.C. *on sidewalk to* ZOOMAN.) Them people were coming in! I heard 'em on the porch! I heard 'em!

REUBEN. (*Bends over the body.*) Be still.

ZOOMAN. Fuck you! I'm Zooman!

(RACHEL, ASH, *and* VICTOR *adlib offstage: Victor, is your father in the room with you? No Mom, I thought he was with you. Rachel, I think I heard shots downstairs. Where's Reuben? Emmett? Etc.*)

ASH. (*Enters* U.L. *crosses down the stairs to* EMMETT.) What happened, Emmett?

EMMETT. I heard 'em tryin' to get in—they were outside the window, screamin' and yellin' (RACHEL *enters* U.L., *crosses down the stairs, crosses to the front door.* VICTOR *enters* U.L., *crosses down the stairs.*)

RACHEL. Reuben? Reuben! (*She opens the door. Crosses onto the porch, crosses* D.S. *down steps to sidewalk.*)

EMMETT. (*Dazed, overlapping.*) It sounded like they were comin' in—(ASH *crosses to the front door, stands on porch in doorway.*) It did to me! (EMMETT *drops the pistol.*)

REUBEN. (*Rises, crosses* S.R. *to porch.*) Call the police—(VICTOR *goes to the phone as* RACHEL *steps toward* REUBEN. REUBEN *crosses* S.L. *to* ZOOMAN, *stands* U.S. *of him.*)

RACHEL. Who is it, Reuben?

REUBEN. Zooman—I heard him yell it.

RACHEL. Zooman? (*She moves forward menacingly.*) This is the one killed my baby? (*To the body.*) Get up! (*She is enraged, but* REUBEN *stops her.*) I'ma kill him! Get up goddamnit!

REUBEN. He's dead, Rachel! (*She struggles to get loose.*)

RACHEL. Let him get up!

REUBEN. He's dead!

RACHEL. Oh, Reuben—oh, my God, Reuben—(REUBEN *puts his arm around her and holds her as she cries.*)

REUBEN. I know, baby. I know.

(*Slowly* REUBEN *starts* RACHEL *back toward the house.* REUBEN *and* RACHEL *enter the house followed by* ASH *as the lights fade out slowly, and another sign is projected on the scrim. It reads: HERE, LESTER JOHNSON WAS KILLED. HE WILL BE MISSED BY FAMILY AND FRIENDS. HE WAS KNOWN AS ZOOMAN. A spotlight builds to brilliance on this new sign, then slowly fades out. The stage goes to black but* ZOOMAN'S *music lingers in the air, mixed with the sound of a distant siren.*)

CURTAIN

ZOOMAN AND THE SIGN

COSTUME PLOT – ACT ONE

REUBEN TATE:

Philadelphia Transit Authority Bus Driver's Uniform
  (no hat)
Same as above, (without hat and jacket)
Same as above *with* hat and jacket

RACHEL TATE:

Striped silk blouse
Brown Skirt
Brown medium heeled sandals

Print house dress
House shoes

Pink night gown
Blue print robe
House shoes

VICTOR TATE:

T-shirt (white with blue sleeves)
Grey corduroy pants
White high topped tennis shoes

EMMETT TATE:

Grey suit

Burgundy tie
Beige shirt

ASH BOSWELL:

Lavender night gown
Lavender robe
House slippers

Same as above
Apron

DONALD JACKSON:

Green plaid work shirt
Brown work pants
Brown construction boots

RUSSELL ODOMS:

Brown/beige 'Ban-Lon' shirt
Blue Jeans
White high top sneakers

ZOOMAN:

Green/white baseball cap
Red t-shirt w/Bison silkscreened on front
Brown corduroy pants
White high topped sneakers
Several gold & silver neck laces

ACT TWO

REUBEN TATE:

Yellow blood stained shirt
Black pants
Khaki jacket

Black suit
Black tie
White shirt
Black shoes
Black socks

T-shirt
Black pants

RACHEL TATE:

Brown print blouse
Brown skirt
Brown purse
Brown medium heeled sandals

Black dress
Black shoes
Black hat
Black gloves
Black purse

Pink night gown
Blue print robe
House shoes

VICTOR TATE:

Grey sweat shirt
Grey pants
Sneakers
White atheletic socks

Black suit
White shirt
Black tie
Black shoes
Black socks

Pajama bottoms
t-shirt

EMMETT TATE:

Striped shirt (torn)
Grey pants

Navy blue suit
Dark blue sling

Yellow shorts
House slippers

ASH BOSWELL:

Blue dress
House slippers

Blue dress
Purse
Medium heeled shoes

Fushia dress
Medium heeled shoes

Lavender night gown
Lavender robe
House slippers

DONALD JACKSON:

Blue plaid work shirt
Brown work pants
Brown construction boots

RUSSELL ODOMS:

Philadelphia 76'ers T- shirt
Blue jeans
sneakers

GRACE GEORGES:

Beige t-shirt
Rust pants
Black sandals

ZOOMAN:

same as Act One

PROP LIST

Switch blade knife	Zooman's props
.22 caliber revolver	Zooman's props
gold necklaces	Zooman's props

5 cans Budweiser beer
Potato peeler
Potato
Bag of groceries
2 bricks
broken glass
Broom
Dustpan
Sling
Plaster of paris cast (for Emmett's forearm)
Guest book
2 loaves of bread
basket (for bread)
Rolled sign
Funeral wreath
Record player
Television
2 Sets of house keys

FURNITURE LIST

CHAIRS—5

1—Down left (below entertainment unit)
1—Up left (next to telephone table)
1—Up center (next to hall table)
1—Stage right (armless)
1—Stage left (left of sofa—matches sofa)

Sofa (seats three)

TABLES—4

1-Up center hall
1-Stage left (telephone)
1-End table (left of sofa)
1-T.V. table

SOUND

All music used in the show reflected the contemporary "disco" sound that is popular today.

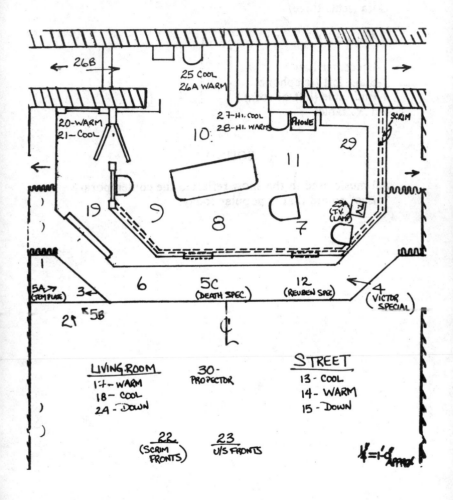

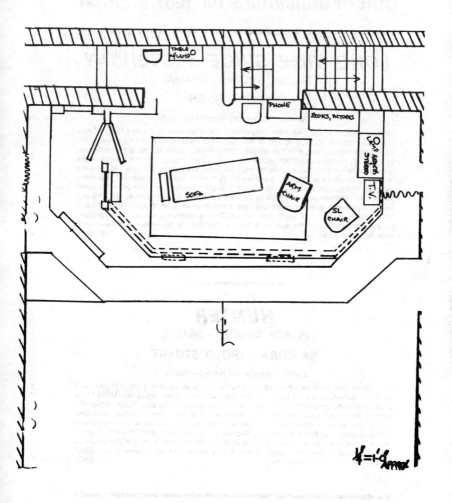

Other Publications for Your Interest

LONG TIME SINCE YESTERDAY
(BLACK GROUPS—DRAMA)
By P.J. GIBSON

8 women—2 Interiors (may be unit set)

Set in suburban Camden, NJ in the early 1980's, this potent new drama by a talented new Black playwright is about a reunion of former college mates, now in their thirties, at the funeral of another friend, who has recently killed herself. These women are prosperous, professional, middle-class Black women who have gone through the turbulence of the sixties and have come out on top in the eighties. These are women you know. At the wake for their sadly deceased friend, the women finally confront the truth about their own lives, and about the suicide which has once again brought them together. All eight roles in the play are well-defined and, needless to say, are quite juicy parts for actresses. This is a literate, humorous, sensitive look at the lives of eight contemporary Black women. It was a SRO success at New York City's New Federal Theatre, which has started so many Black plays and playwrights on the road to recognition. We heartily, fervently recommend *Long Time Since Yesterday.* (#14646)

HUNTER
(BLACK GROUPS—DRAMA)
By NUBA-HAROLD STUART

2 men, 2 women (all blacks)—Interior

This moving and, at times, very humorous new drama is about Jerri, a Black mother, and her new boyfriend, Jake. He has spent the night with Jerri at her house. Jerri fixes him a good down-home breakfast—and introduces him to her teen-aged son, Hunter. Naturally, Jake's pretty surprised to hear that Jerri *has* a son. He is even *more* surprised—and filled with consternation—when Hunter comes to breakfast—for Hunter is severely brain-damaged. Jake then has to make a big decision—just how much does he care for Jerri? This touching new play, a *must* for all college, Black and community theatre groups, was a recent success at New York City's famed Actors Studio. The universality of its subject matter makes *Hunter* a sure winner. (#10162)